Mind Attacks

A JOURNEY FROM HURT TO HEALING

SHEENA MCCULLOUGH

Copyright © 2020 Sheena McCullough

All rights reserved. No part of this publication may be reproduced, distributed, or transmitted in any form or by any means, including photocopying, recording, or other electronic or mechanical methods, without the prior written permission of the publisher, except in the case of brief quotations embodied in critical reviews and certain other noncommercial uses permitted by copyright law.

Paperback ISBN: 978-1-970079-96-8
Hardcover ISBN: 9781636160030
eBook ISBN: 978-1-970079-97-5

Published by Opportune Independent Publishing Company

For permission requests, write to the publisher, addressed "Attention: Permissions Coordinator" to the address below.

Email: Info@opportunepublishing.com

Address: 113 N. Live Oak Street
Houston, TX 77003

Table of Contents

Introduction	9
Acknowledgments	13
Foundation	15
Childhood Trauma	23
Secrets Under The Rug	35
Daddy's Girl	49
Love Connection	57
Sorrow After the Storm	71
From one Hurt to Another	79
Mommy Pleaser To People Pleaser	89
Who are You	95
From Pain to Healing	103
Transformation	111
Epilogue: A Love Letter to Self	117
Hotlines	93
Author bio	95

Dedication

To all the survivors of abuse, my brothers Zuriel and Marshall who inspired me to heal first and manifested this book, thank you!

Mind Attacks

Introduction

Free of false sense of perfections, self-doubt and fear. It is amazing what you are taught to believe from early childhood to adulthood. The constant reminder that I do not have a college degree, which I was told in school was the only way to a successful future. I was inspired by those who could dance, act, or sing, none of which I could do well. I had no idea what my purpose was in this life. One time, I asked my mother what she thought I did well and she responded, "You clean the house very well."

All I could think was I'm going to grow up and be a housekeeper. No way! Not that there is anything wrong with being of service. I knew deep inside my heart it was more to me than just a neat room. I possessed creativity, too. I just hadn't found the thing that I was most passionate about, yet.

Feeling stuck, I wondered will I ever be free to speak my mind; free to dislike what I disliked; free not to get dressed up, fix my hair or put on makeup; free to choose who I like and not feel guilty for who I did not. Can I be free enough to say, "I'm not okay!"

I didn't feel safe to express myself freely, and I didn't know why. There was an aching in my soul that no one knew—a voice unheard. I wondered would anyone miss me if I was dead or would I be forgotten after months had gone by.

I have something to give, something to say. For the first time in my entire life, this is my full voice unapologetic! I've begun a journey of becoming who I was always destined to. Now begins the breaking of old habits and the formation of new. This will be the breaking of generational cycles that prohibited me from speaking my truth. This is my journey on how I fought to overcome anxiety, depression, guilt, and mostly what I like to call "Mind Attacks."

I hope this book will give you hope and inspire you to never give up... to be the voice of change.

Mind Attacks

Replaying past trauma in your mind, staying stagnate in an undeveloped state of being. Traumatized by abuse and suppression of expressing oneself.

Mind Attacks

Acknowledgments

Funny side note (although it wasn't funny at the time). When I first started writing this book, I typed several pages, and none of my work was saved. Talk about frustration!

I wanted to throw my computer against the wall and quit but instead, I called my dearest friend, Marshall. His response to my outburst was, "Well, perhaps you were supposed to tell your story in a different way. You can do it again."

He asked why I felt I couldn't rewrite the pages over again. "I don't want to keep reliving the past hurts," I told him.

He reminded me that I wasn't over all the pain and that I was still in the process of healing. In my mind, I was over it... but I was still scared. I was afraid to let my voice be heard. Even at that very moment, I wanted to scream at him, but I couldn't. Deep inside, I knew he was right.

Mind Attacks

Foundation

Mind Attacks

My parents divorced when I was two years old. Being that young, for a long time I didn't believe the cliché that parents no longer cohabitating would affect me.

My mother remarried when I was five, I will never forget I wore this gold and white shiny dress, and my golden-brown hair in two ponytails. I can't say how I felt, I don't remember. I do remember not knowing anything about him, not being formally introduced, having an undeveloped bond, and feeling a connection with this stranger. But mother was marrying him and I wanted her to be happy.

My mom was a second-generation seamstress and designer, my stepfather was an automotive engineer. One year after they exchanged vows, my mom gave birth to my little brother "Z", that was his nickname. I was extremely happy to have a sibling and he was the cutest thing. He had these big brown eyes and olive skin tone. I knew I wanted to be the best big Sister and to always protect him.

I was raised in a home of strict Christian faith. I was taught not only to preserve my virginity until marriage but, also that this act actually held my value and worth. If I sinned and didn't repent, my spirit would burn in an eternal inferno. As a child, I thought my purpose on Earth was to follow the

Bible's statutes, laws and commandments—"To honor my father and mother," a scripture states.

I started to believe that my own happiness didn't matter, and that life was about making sacrifices. I thought that if I conformed, I would be highly favored and blessed in return. As a child, I never questioned my mother or stepfather, I did as I was told.

Growing up, I was so drawn to helping others. I would help my mom's clients come up with ideas for their outfits and listen to their life stories like women do in beauty shops. I would also chime in when I could to offer my ideas. I would always be complimentary towards them to make them feel beautiful.

In hindsight, I may have involved myself in helping others because it allowed me to escape my own challenges, feel needed, and exalted. I had a very bubbly personality and typically saw the good in everything. I was actively involved in sports and modeling. Since my mother was a seamstress and designed her own fashions, I began walking the runway from a very young age. I enjoyed that time because it allowed for quality time for my mother and I. I became very aware of image at a very young age. While I was growing up, most of my friends were busy being kids while I realized something was different from the way I was being raised. Their parents had corporate jobs, they always wore the latest designer clothing, traveled and their parents gave them an allowance—something my parents did not do. They didn't have to do much to get what they wanted. Unlike my friends, I started working as a fourteen-year-old at a juice and vegan restaurant. One of my close friends, Jazz, and her mom would always talk to me about the importance of education, traveling and trying new things. Her mom didn't feel like working was something Jazz needed to do at all, instead, her focus should only be school and being creative.

Her mom was so affectionate with her too. They gave me something to daydream about. I felt very close to my mom. Beyond any doubt, I knew that she loved me. We talked about everything, but something had gone awry. There was a soul connection but a lack of physical connection. There were no hugs, kisses, or checking on me before I went to bed. There weren't any sweet notes left in my backpack or stroking of my hair. My friends' moms were all affectionate with them. I wanted those things and didn't understand why my mother wasn't that way with me. Later in life, I correlated the fact that she was raised militant, by her father and perhaps she herself lacked in her childhood what I needed in mine.

Growing up, I adapted to my circumstances but

some things weren't what I truly wanted. I tried giving off the impression that I was okay, but the truth is that I wasn't. My support system was very busy with work. In my home, we didn't have sit down dinners, or designated family time.

When I was in grade school, my mom would bring me home from my Grandmother's house, and I couldn't wait to see and talk to her but she would always be talking on the phone with her friends. I'd sit by her side waiting to get a chance to tell her about my day. Sometimes I'd get lucky and she'd get off the phone and talk to me. Other times, I would get tired of waiting. I'm not sure why I never told her how much it bothered me. I'd walk in the door and my stepdad would always be sitting in his beige recliner, patched with silver duct tape to cover the hole forming, watching television. Things were so stagnated; the vibration in the room was so detached.

Everyone was in their own little world and disconnected from one another. My brother always wanted to play the video game, so our connection was disjointed as well. So I would dissolve into my room and listen to music. My favorite artist was Usher, he was my boy crush. So I spent most of my evenings fantasizing about how my life would be with a superstar. The truth was I felt alone. I didn't know how to express how I felt or what I needed from my family.

There is purpose in your pain!

Mind Attacks

Childhood Trauma

Mind Attacks

I remember the distinct smells of old wet towels and wood cleaner that would make your throat itch. I sat in his room, wearing loosely fitted shorts, prickly hair standing up on my scrawny legs, and my hair was sectioned into four ponytails. I was wearing a white shirt, and underneath were my barely formed eight-year-old breasts.

My cousin had invited me into his room to play my favorite video game, "Super Mario." I was so distracted by excitement that I didn't realize he had closed the door behind me. "What other games do you like, cousin?" Dwight asked. "I'll buy them for you."

Innocently, I responded back, "Sonic and Donkey Kong."

I was so excited about the thought of new games! He said, "Come sit in my lap."

We sat on the floor in front of his bed.

I recall him having a full beard, gapped teeth, thick dark hair, weighing approximately two hundred pounds, with child-like hands. I sat between his legs not knowing what he had planned. He wrapped his hands around my waist, playfully teasing me about my belly button. "Cousin, you have an inny (inward belly button)," he said while laughing and tickling me.

Mind Attacks

I giggled a bit but I really wanted to finish playing the game. I started to feel his hands moving from my stomach to my barely grown breasts and then proceeding to tickle me again, this time placing his hand on my legs afterward. He sat there–legs spread wide with me in between them. "I can see your panties cousin, awwh", he said.

I tried to pull my shorts closer to me so he couldn't see. He asked for a kiss on his cheek, and innocently I did it, I just wanted to play the game. "I love you cousin," Dwight said.

By then he moved one hand to my stomach and the other hand was on my thigh. He pulled my shorts and panties away from my body, took his other hand that was on my thigh, and stuck his fingers into my vagina forcefully. I remember a sick feeling in the pit of my stomach that day and many days after.

Immediately, I knew that was not supposed to be happening to me. The smell in the room was nauseating, and I remember feeling nauseous and faint. He used different fingers over and over in my vaginal walls, feeling around like I was an experiment, gripping my thigh and hurting me. He tried kissing me too, but I kept turning my head. Tears rolling down my face, in fear of what he would do next, I clenched my thighs together, telling him, "Stop, please!"

I didn't scream because I was scared.

All I remember is that I dropped the video game controller and everything went black. The next couple of years consisted of constantly looking at myself in the mirror, looking to see if I was okay. I constantly thought about what happened, and it replayed in my head often, even when I tried not to think about it. I call this repetition a "mind attack."

Deep down, I felt super insecure after being molested. I believe I looked in the mirror often in hopes that I would change into someone else. I wanted the thoughts of Dwight to go away and I fell victim to my predator.

During my childhood, my mom would take me to my grandaunt's house so she could care for me while my Mother worked. I loved my grandaunt dearly, she was my grandmother's much older sister.

Molestation happens often with family members whom we never would think would hurt anyone. Every time I would go over there I wanted to play the video game and that was in Dwight's room. I often wonder did my grandaunt know what had happened to me that day. Every time before I would leave her house she would have me lay my head on her lap, while she rubbed my head.

Mind Attacks

She would say, "You're such a sweet little girl."

I wonder, did she know?

I was inherently stuck with unanswered questions and lacked the courage to ever ask.

We used to pray at my grandaunt's house where Dwight lived. His mom, Aunt June, lived there also. We would always pray before I left the house to go home with my mom. Aunt June would laugh in the middle of prayer while speaking in tongues as if she was laughing at the devil. She didn't know the devil was right there in her own home.

I thought that praying would fix everything and make the painful thoughts go away. I hoped that my prayers might even make Dwight go away, and I would be a happy eight-year-old again. But it did not happen.

I wanted to tell my mother but didn't know how, so I asked her a question. I remember being so nervous, scared and confused about how she might respond.

So I asked, "Mommy is it wrong if somebody touches you in your private area?"

She looked at me in complete shock.

Then, she answered and said, "Yes, it is wrong, did somebody do this to you?"

I responded reluctantly and said, "Yes, Dwight did."

Thankfully, she believed me but didn't know what to do, I don't remember her hugging me, but I'd like to think she did. I just remember feeling so scared of what would happen, and who she was going to tell.

I don't remember going to see a doctor either. I believe my mom was afraid to take me, not knowing what would happen if she did. She was left feeling guilty for taking me to my grandaunt's house.

As an adult, she told me that she remembered a time when I was still wearing diapers, and it was time to take a bath.

She sat me in the bathtub but when she cleaned near my private area, I clenched my legs together so tight that she was alarmed and she alerted my Grandmother. It took both of them to separate my legs and finish bathing me.

My mother said she and my Grandmother felt in their heart I had been sexually violated but they didn't know who was doing it. She told me that from the time I was born I would go to my Grand-aunt's house and that she felt deeply this had happened to me long before I was eight years old.

She didn't know it was Dwight because if she did, she would have never allowed me over there.

Of course, being that little I couldn't remember. I was stuck with trying to put the pieces together, but I couldn't. I felt very confused after learning this as an adult. Had I been molested more times than I could remember?

I didn't know and neither did she for sure. There are many physical and psychological effects of sexually abused children.

Research shows that sexually abused children are more likely to develop symptoms of drug abuse, depressive disorders, and post-traumatic stress disorder as an adult and I've had my share.

The way in which my experience has affected my life is post-traumatic stress. In addition, as an adult, I find it difficult to obtain an orgasm or be comfortable sexually. The urge is there but I just cannot let go sometimes, my body rejects my partner. Just when I feel like I am able to, my mind shuts down and my body starts to clinch, and sex begins to feel painful.

A friend of mine also gave me an edible once, thinking it would relax me. Instead I ended up paranoid and grabbing his arm tightly in fear that someone would harm me. I was so upset the next day he drugged me without me knowing. I believe I stored my pain in my subconscious, with triggers that can bring back memories.

Mind Attacks

Your mind doesn't control you!

Mind Attacks

Secrets Under The Rug

Mind Attacks

After telling my mother, she told my father and Grandmother. My Grandmother was so shocked and very upset.

She stopped speaking to her sister after that. She couldn't even bring herself to tell my Grandfather because I think she knew he would have taken Dwight's life and possibly that entire side of the family, being that he was a former marine. Dwight got off without any consequences; he never went to jail or was charged with anything, because my parents didn't proceed with pressing charges. He never apologized or admitted any guilt. My grandaunt protected him, instead of me.

I couldn't believe her reaction—astonished and in disbelief that he would do such a thing.

She always told me how much she loved me and I believed her but suddenly I didn't feel loved at all. I didn't understand why she did not protect me. She chose her grandson over me and that hurt my soul. I felt like a piece of my heart was ripped out of my chest. I felt so betrayed.

My mom didn't take me to see my grandaunt anymore, which made me sad. I loved her so much and felt guilty for not going to visit her, even though she chose her grandson over me. A few years had passed and the last time I saw her she was in the hospital in a coma and died soon after. I cried for a very long time, so many times after her death.

My father was extremely upset and even tried to physically attack Dwight when he learned what happened but my grandaunt begged him not too and stood in the doorway of her house to block him. I remember feeling like it was my fault my family was turned upside down and that none of this would have happened if I didn't say anything.

My mother was in complete shock about everything that was transpiring from my molestation. She never showed when she was sad, never cried to my face, but I knew my molestation hurt her deeply. She did express her frustration with my Grandaunt because she was suppose to watch over me while in her home.

No one asked if I was emotionally okay after being molested nor was I being consoled by anyone I loved so dearly. My mother and I both suppressed our feelings of guilt and I, unfortunately, picked up her coping mechanisms. I tried to forget it ever happened.

I became restrained, refraining from expressing I was deeply saddened and hurt. I begin grieving for several reasons: the loss of my grandaunt, the disappointment and anger my family felt, and the deception I felt.

I became nervous around everyone, biting my nails, especially around anyone who had physical features that were similar to Dwight.

I was easily triggered if someone was too nice or overly interested in me.

I suppressed my feelings and was very sensitive. But like many others with the same experience, I was desensitized, which left me trying to hide my true feelings and just get over it. I thought I was being strong by not showing my hurt.

Then, when I was around ten years old I noticed a pattern between my little brother, who was four at the time, and our cousin. We all stayed together in a two-story spacious home and she and my brother were three years apart so they played together often. She was my stepfather's family member.

I didn't like to play with her much because she was always very rude and mean to me. Even though I was four years older than her, she had a very dominant personality. If I tried to see what she and my brother was doing she would tell me to go away. She was so secretive with him.

I thought she just wanted to make me an outsider, but then I realized she wanted to be alone with him. She used a blanket to cover them up and was her way of blocking my and the rest of the family's view so that we couldn't see what she was doing.

Then one day I saw a fort built of blankets and pillows around them and as I walked up, I saw her hands near his private parts, tickling him and touching him with his underwear and clothing still on. I was shocked and didn't say anything. I just pretended not to notice, but I did plan to keep a close eye on her.

Another time she caught me spying on her while she was playing with my brother and doing the same thing to him and she looked at me and said, "Nobody is going to believe you if you tell." So that let me know then that she knew what she was doing was wrong. It was so hard for me to describe what she was doing because it looked like they were just playing.

However, I knew something wasn't right, it didn't feel right.

Maybe because I had been molested I was on alert, but I felt something and I was determined to make sure my brother was safe. She would constantly isolate herself with my brother and if I tried to come over and play with them, she would make loud outbursts as if I did something to her.

I would get so upset and worried about little my brother. He was so little. I didn't think that I could explain to him why she shouldn't be playing with him like that, so I didn't. Then one Summer we took a family road trip to New Orleans to visit my stepfather's parents. We rented a van so all of us could fit, and low and behold that was the worse drive ever.

Our cousin wanted to sit next to my brother of course and the whole drive she snickered at me, as if to let me know she was in control and my brother was all hers. I knew I had to do something, so I told my mother on the drive there while on a restroom break, what was happening to my brother.

She saw how upset I was and she believed me. My mom was outraged and told me that she was going to talk to my stepfather about it and she did. It wasn't that alarming that my stepfather's response was dismissive. He felt like since his family member was a child she was unaware of what she was doing to my brother. Often times this happens in children to children sexual abuse.

The behavior is excused and looked at like the child is just curious, however I believe this is the start of forming bad habits. When we reached New Orleans at our grandparents' home, my mom was fuming hot and she confronted her mother, instead of waiting on my stepfather to address the situation. She immediately said that I was lying. They all got into a big argument but our Grandparents did not want to hear of it. In the old days molestation and abuse was swept under the rug, never to be spoke of again.

I was upset and hurt, I didn't understand why her mother felt I would lie. I truly felt like an outcast. I didn't hate our cousin, I just wanted her to STOP.

Nothing happened to her; instead, we separated as a family, not speaking about it ever again. Once again, I felt responsible for causing a rift in the family. As a result, I became very quiet and felt misunderstood. More importantly, I felt like I didn't do a good job of protecting my brother and that broke my heart. I was only looking at the negative side of things—everyone being upset.

Again, I witnessed absolutely no consequences for this type of bad behavior.

I felt like I hadn't resolved anything, but instead, I caused something much worse. However, when I became an adult, my mother disclosed that her mother knew her daughter was being inappropriate and she actually did believe me because during their confrontation in New Orleans she finally admitted it. She saw those habits in her daughter but had been ignoring it.

Now I understand the embarrassment something like this could have caused but what about the effects nothing being done had on all parties involved.

My brother grew up to resent his father's side of the family. As an adult, he discussed how he felt to our Mother and I. I realized my little brother and I were remarkably similar. We both endured unresolved pain and were both holding on to it. As time passed, my cousin and her mother started coming back around again as if nothing ever happened.

My brother and I never received an apology or even an acknowledgment of what happened. Maybe our parents let it go, but again we were stuck with feeling alone and unprotected. It wasn't fair, the adults made up but what about my brother and my feelings.

I thought he wouldn't remember as we grew up, but he remembered everything. He expressed how it's stifled his relationships with women, he doesn't like it if a woman is too aggressive.

Reason being, his first time sexually wasn't a pleasurable experience at all. I realized that just because time passes doesn't mean our pain will be healed. The pain has to be addressed and not hidden or looked over.

Mind Attacks

I blamed myself for many years for my brother's introverted ways, I thought if only I beat her up or showed him I could stop her myself, he would have a different outlook as an adult.

It wasn't until much later into my adult life that I realized I was holding onto guilt and I had to let it go. I prayed about my feelings and I asked my brother if he blamed me at all for not protecting him or for speaking up about what I saw and he said no, he didn't blame me at all.

He resented our parents for still allowing them to come around us. I'll never forget when he was graduating from college, my aunt was there to congratulate him. However, I think what he really needed was a sincere apology.

I know he appreciated the support but I believe he would have liked to have a real heart-to-heart instead. To this day my brother is still silencing his pain. I thank my Heavenly Father he opened up to my mother and me, but he still needs to share his truth with whomever he chooses, perhaps he will in time.

My mother, on the other hand, got a divorce when my brother was twelve and I was eighteen. I didn't exactly know her complete reasoning but she explained to me that she was very depressed and knew if she didn't leave things would get worse. She felt like he was detached from reality, and was not a good protector or provider.

His condescending ways had finally caught up to her. She even started feeling suicidal before leaving and divorcing him. She described it as feeling as though she failed.

Often time, victims of any sort of abuse protect their abusers. I'm not sure as to why but perhaps it could be because of the responses of others if the truth was told. The fear of rejection or being misunderstood is something we all dare to conquer.

Mind Attacks

Speak your truth even when afraid!

Mind Attacks

Daddy's Girl

Mind Attacks

My father was a very disciplined man; he worked at the Post office, drove luxury cars, and always kept himself looking sharp. He was tall and very fit. Early on, I learned he was very attractive to women. Women would always say it to me or to someone else around me. I looked at my father from a completely different view; I admired him so much because he always seemed so peaceful and humble.

As a child, he was always affectionate, hugging and kissing me. He was the first man I ever loved. He came to visit me a few times a month and called me regularly, but it wasn't as much as I needed. When I spent time with him I felt safe. Although he wanted me to confide in him, I found it difficult to share my life stories.

I wanted my father to be proud of me because I'm his only child. I believe I put this pressure on myself to be a certain way with him because I wanted his approval. I questioned if I was good enough to be "Daddy's girl."

Even though he always said he loved me, I didn't feel I was worthy to be loved by someone who was so well-liked.

I felt embarrassed that I was molested. I was so used to fighting to be heard, for affection and attention from my mother's side of the family. I realized later that I did not know how to accept affection when it was given freely to me from my Dad.

I knew my father loved me, but I couldn't explain the shame I felt to him or anyone else. Perhaps it would have been different if my Dad had talked to me about being molested and if he reassured me it wasn't my fault and that I was going to be okay.

I think parents often are dealing with their own emotions in situations that it's easy to forget about the child's emotional needs.

Outwardly, it may seem like a child is okay and moving forward in life, but the truth is there can be so many feelings unaddressed on the inside.

I was processing through the pain in a very very lonely way. Memories of Dwight often played in my head.

The *Mind Attacks* made me truly traumatized. I doubted myself in decisions constantly. As a result, I became even more indecisive.

My stepfather was a very dominant figure in my life. Our relationship was an autocracy. He took great interest in my hobbies and was obliged to take me places with my friends. As long as I did as I was told, everything was okay.

But if I didn't want to do something there was a lot of discussion and persuasion as to why I should see things his way. Once, when I was thirteen, I was in an argument with my maternal grandfather. My stepfather wanted me to just be quiet, so as I stormed down the hallway, he followed right behind me.

He grabbed me by my neck and hit me on my head with his fist. I was shocked and scared of what he would do if I rebelled against him ever again. I immediately told my mother, but sadly she didn't know whom to believe. He denied it and said I was exaggerating.

My mom did not question him or say anything else about it to me. I felt so betrayed, I felt like my feelings weren't validated. She didn't ask me if I was okay, even later after things had cooled off.

I remember going to school the next day and telling my friends what had happened. I was so hurt because my mom said nothing. As a result, even more anger and resentment started to build up inside of me.

I felt like my own home was no longer a place of safety and refuge. So, I tried to spent more and more time away. I found peace while at different friends' houses. Most of my friends were guys; we were like family. The way my neighborhood was set up, everybody knew each other. My male friends told me to not trust people and they had my back. We formed a pack, and I became a part of their gang.

I had protection now and that made me feel untouchable.

I was untouchable from the people like my cousin in the world and from my lying stepfather. They made me feel safe and important.

We were our own family and they protected me in school and in the streets. My parents started noticing I would get into physical fights, and I wasn't remorseful for it. I actually liked to fight. Nobody was ever going to hurt me again. I felt like I had the protection I longed for from my parents.

My behavior was unacceptable to my family so my parents decided to send me to a different high school, away from my friends, and where my stepfather's family member worked. This was their attempt to save me from my bad behavior. I resented them for making me go to Crenshaw High School, but in the end, I adjusted and made new friends.

My mistrust of people slowly started to change. I started to like my new school and peers.

My connection with people started to open. I was dating guys and living a pretty normal teenage life. I didn't get into any fights or have problems at Crenshaw High.

I was a bit timid at times but I had people who understood my shyness and would make me laugh. I went on to graduate from high school on the B honor roll, then attended a junior college. I was accepted into a university but my parents said it would be too expensive.

I became very interested in the arts, enrolled in classes like speech, dance, and acting. I loved fashion, which wasn't a coincidence, and decided to major in fashion merchandising and buying.

I worked at Nordstrom at the time, which I loved and even took my first trip out of the country with my school to Europe. Yes Europe, we traveled to Paris, Switzerland, Monaco and Nice. College opened my eyes to a whole new world of culture, beliefs and opportunities. It was a blessing to be afforded the opportunity to participate in new things.

I greatly appreciated my mother for paying for me to go to Europe, she sacrificed to make that happen, working extra jobs. I came back to the States with a whole new perspective on life. I was full of optimism and ready to define my place in the world.

Love Connection

Mind Attacks

It was my twenty-first birthday, and my friends, family and new boyfriend surprised me with a party in the backyard of my Grandma's house. I walked in wearing a green terry cloth dress, hair straight down to my shoulders, with the biggest smile on my face. I felt so happy to see everyone I cared about so much there to celebrate me.

The only one missing was my Grandmother. She was in a nursing home trying to recover from a stroke she had previously. She was my biggest supporter and loved me unconditionally. Despite the fact of her not being there, that birthday will always be one of the most memorable and special to me. It was a happy time for me.

I was madly in love with my boyfriend, Kevin that I knew from grade school. We remained in touch throughout our school day years. He came all the way from Mississippi to be there for my birthday and that made me feel so special. We became extremely passionate, spending as much time as we could with one another and becoming sexually involved with one another unprotected. He made me feel so good.

I felt a very very deep connection with him for several reasons. First, being his parents weren't together and second, he was verbally abused as a child growing up and felt very alienated. We had something in common—brokenness.

Mind Attacks

We were emotionally wrecked.

We discussed our past and the future often, but in hindsight, I should have asked him way more questions. There was a lot we didn't know about each other and would soon find out. A couple of months after my birthday, I hadn't even been out to a nightclub yet or had my first shot of tequila.

I had missed my period. I was so scared at the thought of being pregnant. At that very moment all I could think about was, what will my parents say? And how disappointed they would be if I were pregnant. Scared is an understatement, I felt terrified. Telling Kevin I thought I was pregnant wasn't the easiest either. I didn't know how he was going to react, but my mother had warned me as a teenager that most boys flee when finding out a girl is pregnant.

I told Kevin I was pregnant, he seemed surprised but not upset, he said, "Take a test and make sure." So we went to the store and came back to my house while my parents were at work and I took the test.

We both sat there in fear of a positive result.

I sat there thinking about what this would mean for my life, everything would change but there also was this part of me that was smiling on the inside. A little bundle of joy could be forming in my womb.

We placed the test on the counter, holding our breath in anticipation and then boom, our whole world changed, two pink lines, it was POSITIVE!

I knew there was no doubt that I was going to keep my baby, but Kevin on the other hand asked me, "What are you going to do?"

He felt we were not ready to have a child because we were too young. I didn't care, I was going to get ready and that's just what I did. I told Kevin if he wanted to go back to Mississippi then go, I was willing to figure out things on my own.

I didn't realize it, but at that very moment, I released him of all responsibility, all the love I thought he had for me suddenly changed in my mind to he wasn't going to be there for me.

So I somehow thought I was going to one up him by dismissing him from fatherhood at the beginning. As I mentioned before in my religious belief I was not supposed to be having sex out of wedlock. My parents had never discussed the importance of condoms and protection. I wasn't supposed to be having sex, period.

Also, I was never told how important it was to

ask questions before entering into a relationship sexually. Knowing how your partner feels about having children is important, what age do they see themselves doing so, how many kids they want, what do they plan to do in order to take care of their family career wise. These are the things I should have known already but there I was possibly pregnant.

We went to the doctor's office to confirm what we already knew to be true. The hardest step was telling my mom. I felt the need to tell her a certain way, just like I had done when I was eight. This time being older and more clever, I called her and asked her to take a car ride with me. My head was spinning about how to tell her that I was pregnant. I did the only thing I could think of doing—put the ultrasound on her lap. "I know what this is," she said.

Starring at me, she told me to give her some time to digest and she got out the car. She wasn't upset to my knowledge but definitely astonished. A few days went by and then reality set in that she was going to be a Grandma. I knew and felt in my heart she was going to be there for my unborn baby and me, and she was indeed.

My father's reaction was quite surprising, my son was going to be due in April and my dad's birthday was on April 24th. I told him over the phone, his response was, "This is going to be the best birthday gift ever."

I was so thrilled to have both my parents' support. Kevin's parents, however, were in two totally different States. His father lived in the same city I did and his mother was in Mississippi. Kevin's intention was just to visit for the Summer prior to the pregnancy and then he would go back home with his mother. His relationship with his father was not stable so he didn't reach out for support like I did with my parents.

Once he overstood I was not having an abortion he decided he would have to figure out a way to stay in California. So we asked my mom and stepdad could he stay with us. Against my parents' religious beliefs, they allowed it, but not without commitments.

My stepfather started pressuring us to do the "right thing" and get married, like scripture says. We both felt we weren't ready, but at the same time I wanted to satisfy my family, especially my mom.

I felt I had disobeyed God, having sex before marriage, and now having a child out of wedlock, so in my heart I wanted to restore my goodness with God. I just knew Kevin was going to leave. I pictured him catching the quickest train back to

Mississippi.

But he didn't leave to my surprise, he stayed with us. That spring I gave birth to our son and a year later we said our vows before God at city hall in Los Angeles.

We didn't have a big wedding, even though I wanted to. My father didn't walk me down the aisle; I didn't even tell him I was getting married that day. I'm not sure as to why, but I remember later my father feeling very hurt I did not invite him. The truth was it was not how I planned. Of course, I wanted my father to walk me down the aisle, but not at city hall. I did what I was told to do, not what I wanted to.

I became very servile in my relationship with Kevin too. If it were completely up to me, Kevin and I would have taken our time. We wouldn't have rushed into marriage.

I remember wanting to have a big wedding with all my friends and family there but my close friends, like Jazz, weren't too happy I was getting married so young. In their eyes, I should have been single while in college, and focusing on my career dreams. So with that being said, I just thought the courthouse was best, with my mom, grandmother, stepfather and my one-year-old son.

I just wanted to be happy and make my parents proud. After all, they told my son's father and I it was the Godly thing to do. Deep down I had always dreamed of finishing college and getting married later on in life but sometimes life goes a different way.

My husband and I looked like the perfect couple. We always dressed to impress. He was charming and funny. We even started bringing our son around my in-laws. I got along well with his father, stepmother and sisters. They would even babysit our son, which was helpful. Both of our families were very involved and opinionated towards my husband and our relationship.

Kevin was very uncomfortable with how much they were in our business, so I started isolating myself more. He would say he didn't trust anyone and since he didn't have the best relationship with either of his parents he didn't understand the relationship I had with mine.

I tried to overcompensate with love and doing things for him and I encouraged my family to do so also. However, that wasn't enough.

Our relationship deteriorated and things got to a point where his pain became greater than our love. Nothing I did was good enough. Something in his character changed drastically for the worse.

Mind Attacks

He became very mean not too long after getting married. I would try to talk to him and he would shut me out.

He became so argumentative about anything. I began to feel like I was walking on eggshells. He became impulsive, drinking and smoking weed often. I remember one day while at home he told me, "I don't have to be with you, Bitch. I don't need you or anyone. Fuck you, Bitch."

I didn't know if I was coming home to him being high, angry or in the mood to have sex.

Usually, he would pick a fight, and then apologize during sex, and then the next day figure out a reason to leave for days at a time. The sad part was, I would accept him when he came back.

I would question him about his whereabouts, but he would yell so much that I would try to calm him down and satisfy him any way I could. I wanted him and accepted him in spite of the things he said and the way he treated me.

The verbal attacks continued and got worse. I started feeling like I didn't want to live anymore because I was so unhappy.

Suicide is the tenth leading cause of death in the United States, according to USA Today. In 2018,

48,344 Americans died by suicide. I definitely felt like I didn't want to live like that anymore, but I didn't want to leave him either.

One night, when my son was three years old, he watched his father choke me while the two of us argued over me talking to a platonic male friend.

I was so scared of what he would do next. I stayed quiet and just wanted him to leave, and he did... like a coward. I also recall another time we had a disagreement while picking up fast food. He got so upset that he threw the food everywhere; it was flying all over the car and on my face. The disrespect was constant.

I felt so depressed and had nobody to turn to. I now understand he was insecure.

Knowing that my child witnessed such violence from his father toward me, I knew I had to get out of the marriage. Feeling humiliated, I didn't tell my family or any friends what was happening in my marriage.

I think I had picked up my husband's habits of blocking people out. I didn't want anyone to place blame on him or judge me.

I had lost myself completely.

Mind Attacks

We stayed together for nearly five years, but I couldn't tolerate the pain of our broken marriage anymore. I asked him to go stay at his cousin's house. He responded, "If I leave, I'm not coming back." And he kept his word, he never returned.

Be fearless & unashamed!

Mind Attacks

Sorrow After the Storm

Mind Attacks

I don't know what hurt more, the abuse or him leaving. I mourned our divorce like a person mourns a loved one's death. Again, I grieved in silence.

I felt as though a part of my soul was gone and I had failed as a wife and lost my best friend. I filed for divorce and physical custody of our son, because I knew it was the best choice. I didn't want my son to be raised in a toxic environment. He didn't deserve that and neither did I.

The adjustment from a two-parent home to a single parent home was not easy. I worked two jobs at times to afford the expenses of my son and I. Surely, I was filled with so much sadness and resentment towards my ex-husband. I was heartbroken.

Unknowingly, I started taking my emotions out on my son. He was named after his father. I was so upset about getting married and that it ended as a failure. The deep anger I felt within me caused me to yell at my son when he wouldn't obey quickly enough or do what I told him to do. I was easily agitated.

He would laugh when I got upset too, and that would make me even more angry.

I found it difficult to balance my spiritual, home,

Mind Attacks

work and social life.

I would attend church regularly every Sunday and bible study once a week. I prayed for strength, and asked God why he would let all that happen to me. I didn't understand why my marriage didn't work out and why I wasn't loved right. I tried to do what I was taught was right.

I didn't know how to handle the pressure and uncertainty of raising a child by myself. I suffered from anxiety and panic attacks. The truth is, I was falling apart on the inside.

I thought about committing suicide a few times, but I was taught that my spirit would burn in eternal ferno if I ended my own life. I also did not want to leave my son; he gave me a reason to live and I loved him more than anything.

I decided to take leave from work and undergo therapy. In black communities, we often ignore mental health. Let's face it, in our culture we are often taught to pray about our problems and go to church. I had been there and done that.

I prayed, confessed my sins, and asked for forgiveness, but I still wasn't okay, I still felt broken, betrayed, alone, and tired.

So, I decided after several doctor's appointments

for stress and anxiety, that it was best that I saw a therapist.

It was then I learned how to process through the pain and I began to heal. After several sessions alone, I then brought my son. I learned how disappointed and upset he was that his father left, how sad and scared he felt when I yelled, and that he remembered his father choked me. It broke my heart to see my son so hurt from this.

Therapy did help us understand one another better. It changed our lives! For the first time, I saw myself, and I did not like who I had become. I learned that the first step in resolving hurt is acknowledging it.

I had to own my mistakes and then look my son in the face and apologize for everything I did to him and for not being the mother he deserved, and I did. He did not deserve my bad actions and behavior. My son forgave me, and I forgave myself for taking my hurt out on him.

I was being too demanding and critical of him, just like my ex-husband had been toward me. From that day forward, I made an agreement with him. I promised not to yell at him, and instead be open with how I was feeling and to listen to him and keep track of how he was feeling. To this day, we constantly check in with each other and our bond is stronger than ever.

I learned then what it meant to have a panic attack. My heart would palpitate quickly and I would think I was about to pass out. In the beginning, I tried a low dose anxiety medication. But during therapy I learned that when that happens, I was shallow breathing.

I became very cautious of my breathing, and I still monitor myself, sometimes I have to stop and focus on every breath. I began to feel better and returned back to work after several weeks of treatment. I felt stronger and more hopeful about our future. I realized the importance of asking for help.

Your bad choices are not a measurement of your true ability!

Mind Attacks

From one Hurt to Another

Mind Attacks

After a couple of years, I started dating again. My dating life was more down than up; I just could not seem to get the consistency I wanted in a man. I would fall in and out of love, resulting in heartbreak after heartbreak. I think the worst part about it is going through it feeling alone.

I had my share of doing things I shouldn't have as an adult. Some of which I was never caught, and the time I did get in trouble it started with me visiting my childhood friend that was locked up in prison, serving a life sentence. I became co-dependent on him.

After years of visiting him and falling crazy in love, he sexually forced me to do something I did not want to do in the open. Doing so, resulted in me getting arrested. Thankfully, I got a slap on the wrist and only had to pay a fine, with the condition of not getting in trouble again. I learned a valuable lesson. He used my vulnerability and desire for love and connection against me. I thought it was love, and I wanted it to be. Instead, I felt embarrassed and stupid for falling victim again to such bad and low vibration habits.

I resented my heart for loving too much. I think the worse feeling was loving a man that didn't love me the way I needed to be loved, and the worst part was that I couldn't even tell him what I needed because I didn't know myself.

Mind Attacks

I hated being vulnerable.

I was lonely, and instead of focusing on myself I was looking for a man to take all my problems away. Unknowingly, I kept attracting men who were broken like me. I was so used to being hurt that I had allowed pain to become my normal. Engaging in activities that did not serve me, doing things, I would not normally do to please my lover, trying hard to prove that I was worthy of love and settling. Although I hadn't had many partners, I had toxic relationships.

I hated dating and my friends would say it should be fun. It's funny, I told my girlfriends I accepted being single for the rest of my life and they reassured me I wouldn't be forever. They were right, there was one guy that I met at a mutual friends birthday party, during a game of speed dating. He was everything my ex-husband wasn't; he traveled, was intelligent, an entrepreneur, no kids and handsome. In the beginning of our courtship, he was ending a relationship. I was not down to just hook up sexually and I expressed that to him.

He became available quickly and we became a couple. I introduced him to my son and family. I learned so much from him. I appreciated our long talks, nights watching documentaries and making love.

He was everything I thought I wanted but part of me still felt something was missing. Have you ever experienced being in love with someone who doesn't love you the same? That's just what happened in this relationship.

Every person on Earth has his or her own love language, mine were words of affirmation. I have been able to identify the love languages of others and give them the love they seek, but I struggle to receive the love I desire in return.

At one point, my heart simply felt numb toward him. Although he said I was beautiful, and he loved me, I did not believe him. I may have tricked myself to thinking I was in love, but deep down I knew he was not and neither was I. It had been lust, not love. I figured that out when I would listen to all of his goals and aspirations, but he wasn't ever interested in mine.

I was afraid of ending up alone. I gave so much energy to our relationship and little to myself. Mentally, I was exhausted and tired of not being important to the people I loved, including him. I was let down by having certain expectations in my relationship, thinking he would do certain things, but very afraid to say what I wanted.
It began to feel forced. I blamed myself instead of talking to him and being honest. Why is it that we always blame ourselves? I was not happy in our

relationship and his desires of me were more than I could give.

I did not know what to expect from men, because nobody ever told me. He ended the relationship with me first because of a career choice I made. We tried to work through our differences, but it failed so we went our separate ways. I had to come to terms with myself, that I was not the one for him or maybe anyone.

I was tired of trying to figure out if I was good enough and prove myself worthy of love. It didn't help towards the end of the relationship when he started pointing out all the bad things he felt toward me.

He downplayed my new career move, as if I was worthless and constantly reminded me of how it messed up our relationship. He blamed me for everything. He said my job was worthless, that I was nobody, and without him, I would fail.

I started feeling depressed, but this time I didn't shut myself off from my family and friends.

Instead, I opened up about my break-up. Thank goodness for my friends that I could trust and be open with.

They helped me see it was not my fault; I had

no control over the decision he made to break up. After the breakup, I learned to control my thoughts by writing down positive affirmations. Every time I'd have a mind attack or was around someone who was being negative, I thought of something that maked me smile or happy.

I challenged myself to write something positive in order to counteract that thought.

For example:

Negative thought: *He doesn't really like you.*

Mind transformation: *I am loved, and I am enough.*

Negative thought: *You are not smart enough to be an author.*

Mind transformation: *My book is going to help someone.*

Negative thought: *You don't have enough money.*

Mind transformation: *I saved $100 last week not eating out.*

Speaking affirmations became a part of my everyday routine, in the mornings before I started my day. I accepted the role I played in making bad choices. I needed to spend time simply being alone.

Mind Attacks

No man or friend could heal me or save me; I had to save myself. I had to reflect on what I had gone through and where I was going to end up if I didn't change my habits.

Healing for me was about accepting my past and forgiving myself first, then others. I began to write love letters to myself, I also started reading self-help books more.

I found this really mind-opening book called, "The Artist Way" by Julia Cameron, which suggested I start writing as soon as I open my eyes in the morning. I would write whatever my heart desired. It is vital that we learn how to love ourselves and accept ourselves as human beings who are constantly growing in awareness. If pain is not acknowledged as a child, you will grow up as an adult still having that pain held inside as a child and carry that into new relationships.

I wanted to be free. I no longer wanted to be an adult with unresolved trauma. I wanted better for myself. I had to acknowledge my truth. I began a new journey of becoming whole, and it wouldn't be easy.

Sheryl I. Spiller said, "You have to bloom where you are planted."

I couldn't agree more.

Mind Attacks

Mommy Pleaser to People Pleaser

Mind Attacks

We really can be our own worst critics.

Our environment and experiences can shape the thoughts we have about ourselves. For this reason, being in constant awareness is key.

People's perception of us also plays a huge part in our lives. It is the people closest to us that have the strongest impact on our thought processes, actions, and reactions. Even in the wholeness of speaking positive affirmations, old ways can resurface. It's our own responsibility to recognize the source. I had to look deeper into who influenced me the most.

My mom is one of the closest and dearest people in my life; we support each other through every triumph. She is my role model. Her independent ways and business endeavors taught me the meaning of strength. She is why I kept moving forward in life and could not give up. This is the main woman in my life I always wanted to please.

A pivotal time in my life was when our house caught fire. We encountered problems with the contractor. My mother and I would often end up yelling at each other instead of talking about how things should be done. It was a very chaotic time for us. When my mother was upset she'd become sarcastic.

However, I learned a very important thing: my communication was broken in difficult times and perhaps hers was too. I realized we never argued because I never really disagreed with her about anything.

I began to reflect and remembered that during my childhood I didn't like to disagree with anyone. Confrontation equaled fighting, resulting in me silencing my voice. I wanted everyone I came into contact with to be happy. I wanted to please my entire family.

I realized I was carrying a huge weight I put upon myself. I was a "people pleaser." I wasn't making decisions on my own terms but instead, I was basing it off of how it would affect others. Not only in my romantic relationships had I become servile, but in my family relationships as well.

I was still holding on to bad habits and feelings of being unheard or misunderstood. I was holding my own self prisoner to my own freedom. I began to see a pattern in my life and not a good one. I desired to reach a point where I didn't care what others thought of me.

I realized I felt insignificant and this was a cycle I repeated often. I didn't like myself. I wanted to be strong. I prayed for God to change me and make me over. I asked God to retract the idea I made up in my mind as a child, that my purpose in life was to sacrifice my own happiness. I didn't want to be a people pleaser anymore but rather a presence felt.

Mind Attacks

Who are You?

Mind Attacks

I remember the first time I sat down with a client, whom I worked for as a personal assistant, he asked me, "Who are you? Tell me about yourself."

I sat there puzzled. I couldn't think of anything to say. All I kept thinking was that I am nothing more than a person who's never did anything I wanted to do. I was a people pleaser.

He obviously could see by my facial expression I didn't know. So, then he asked, "Well, who do you want to become?"

At that time, my mind couldn't think beyond the fact that I was a twenty-eight-year-old single mother with nothing in my mind that I wanted to accomplish. When I was growing up, I wanted to be a model or an actress. Jada Pinkett and Nia Long inspired me. I could see myself on camera back then. I tried acting school but I didn't have the money or transportation to keep going.

You would think it would be easy being that I was born and raised in Los Angeles. The truth is, I lived in L.A. my whole life, but I did not have the Los Angeles experience.

I was stuck in the hamster wheel of corporate America, going around and going nowhere, living at home with my mom.

Mind Attacks

I was afraid to admit to my new client that I didn't have my life figured out. Despite being unable to answer his questions, he still hired me to keep him organized and put his life back together. How would it sound, me saying I don't have my life figured out?

I knew one thing, the next time someone asked me that question, I would be able to answer it strongly. I set out a goal to find myself. I began traveling to places I had only dreamed about but could never afford, staying at the best hotels, dining at expensive restaurants, and being able to afford designer clothing and shop at places I'd only seen in magazines.

I no longer had to bargain shop. My life became fun, spontaneous, and worth living. I was even able to afford a nanny when I was traveling for weeks at a time.

My client had many late nights at the studio and nightclubs, and I would wake him up in the morning (after he'd had several bottles of patron the previous night), check his emails, and schedule photo shoots and hosting appearances.

I was very important to him.

My life became entangled in his life and I did not mind it. It was another escape from my own woes and after a while, I started thinking it couldn't get any better than this.

After almost six years of working for my client, business bookings started to slow down, and I was forced to go back to working in corporate America. As you can imagine, the shift was very disturbing. I appreciated my job, it allowed me to be able to save some money and take care of my responsibilities but I also had other dreams.

At 6:30 a.m., I would force myself to get up and get ready to start work at 8:30 a.m. On a good day, I would have enough time to meditate, pray and then begin my day.

My boss had already warned me that if I called in sick one more time, I would be fired. The truth was I was mentally tired, and I'm not quite sure from what exactly. My mind was at war with what I had been told my whole life: get a stable job with benefits and that's all you need. But I was feeling more and more that I was born to create.

It was as if I was missing something in my life once again.

I felt so routine and I was lacking passion. "Who are you?" I asked myself.

When I thought about what made me happy, or

gave me a sense of peace, one thing stood out in my mind— writing.

My inner voice was telling me, I am a voice, a writer, and a visionary. I am a woman who stands on faith and knows how to carry out her purpose. I practice loving myself, meditating, and living in my highest self, I treasured my alone time. My voice is an expression of love, truth, and passion.

I am whole and complete, resulting in acts of kindness to others. I love effortlessly. I carry a journal of knowledge; I am mindful, strong and no longer mind attacked without power.

I made the decision to believe in myself and start a new journey of passion writing. I continued working during the day and started writing at night. I began to find myself. Writing helped me to become a better person, a better woman.

I am not the cause of anybody else's Inadequacies!

Mind Attacks

From Pain to Healing

Mind Attacks

I am now where I'm supposed to be. I am in love with myself.

I have the power to shift the atmosphere and be that change. I realize I will never stop healing. I'd like to think that everything we go through is a process. Some pain we may never forget, but we must learn the lessons from it.

I didn't find healing from being molested until much later in life, but it's never too late.

I started to heal when my dear friend Marshall once asked, "Have you prayed for Dwight and forgiven him?"

Truly, I was just happy he was dead. I'm not sure what he died from but I really didn't care. Why do I need to pray for him? I said.

Marshall said, "You are praying for him, for you."

I sat there puzzled and angry and not quite sure how to respond. "Are you ready to let go?" he asked.

My friend guided me in prayer but first, he told me not to repeat after him, unless I meant it. I agreed.

Mind Attacks

The prayer went like this:

Creator of heaven and Earth, I forgive.
I forgive Dwight for molesting me.
I forgive myself for blacking out and not remembering all that happened.
I pray for his soul and for the creator of this Earth to have mercy on him.
I forgive my mother for not being able to protect me.
I forgive my father for not being able to protect me.
I forgive my grandaunt for possibly knowing Dwight was molesting me.

Please understand this was very difficult to do. Every time I forgave, I began to take what seemed like a new breath of life. Tears filled my eyes and my inner scars started to heal. I never thought, twenty years after the trauma, I would ever revisit this pain again and find healing.

There was one more thing Marshall had me do and it blew my mind. He said, "I want you to lie down, close your eyes, and picture yourself as your eight-year-old self, back at the house with Dwight."

He paused for a moment. "Do you see her?" he

asked.

I responded, "Yes."

I could see myself wearing loosely fitted shorts and my white shirt sitting on the floor playing a video game while Dwight was sitting behind me with his legs open, bringing me closer to his lap.

Marshall asked me, "What would you say to that eight-year-old little girl?"

I sat there feeling full of emotions, thinking of all the things that happened that day. Sadness and tears begin to fill my eyes. I said, "It's not your fault he hurt you! What happened to you doesn't define who you will become. You are enough! Do not let anyone make you feel you are unworthy of love. Don't let anyone take your smile away.

This monster does not win! You have already won as long as you don't quit. You will have bad days and good days, but you can choose to see the good. I love you and remember to let your voice be heard."

I began to hug her and when I opened my eyes, I was hugging myself. More tears filled my eyes as I began to pour love into myself.

Marshall explained that I was here in this body

of a grown woman yet stuck with the pain from when I was eight years old.

With this experience of forgiveness and honesty, I took my power back. I freed her.

I can't tell you enough how this changed my life.

I remembered who I was...

Before the *Mind Attacks*, physical attacks, and sexual abuse ever took place.

I remembered me!

*You are the writer of
your own story!*

Mind Attacks

Transformation

Mind Attacks

Butterflies

Before a butterfly becomes a beautiful creature, it must go through a metamorphosis. It's uncomfortable in a cocoon, all wet and slimy with no space to move. It must go through four different stages before it reaches adulthood and a new life begins. My new life began when I embraced the discomfort and pain of my past. And I chose to forgive. Only then was I able to transform into an unmistakable version of myself.

I didn't quit in the early stages of my new found development. Speaking positive affirmations and finding my voice within allowed me to recognize my true self.

Undoubtedly, I am more than just a caterpillar. It was necessary to go into a cocoon to protect my energy and space.

I had to be patient in my metamorphosis. I was faced with challenges and had to overcome fear.

I had to finally stop blaming others for my repetitive actions, for not being what I wanted it to be or doing what I wanted to do. I was the only one stopping me; it wasn't my past circumstances.

Before I was afraid, negative thoughts would fill my mind and totally discourage me, but now I am

Mind Attacks

in control of my thoughts.

Writing has been my refuge, my place of peace. It has become my voice, strength, and a place where I feel unjudged.

I stopped believing in a false reality and started walking in my truth. I practiced showing gratitude instead of a bad attitude. Things began to change for the better. I had a dream once that a big white truck maliciously hit me, while I was standing in my driveway. I couldn't see inside the front windshield to see who it was, but the truck came right at me and killed me. Once I woke up, I searched online and looked up what the dream might have meant, it suggested that I am continuously trying to measure up to others.

After this, I made the decision to put something else to rest, instead of myself. All of the pain, guilt, resentment, confusion and shame were demolished and I am now free like a butterfly.

I am a living testimony that your life can change but that change must start within self. I choose to be victorious and not a victim of my past. Now I am actively managing my mind and my attacks. I feel more positive and aligned than ever before.

I'm thankful that you've chosen to take the time to read my journey.

I pray that my heart reaches you in this moment. My last thought: find the sweet in your sour. There is beauty even in the darkness because your heart is beating there, and you are the light waiting to burst through.

Thank you for allowing me to share my mind with you.

Mind Attacks

Epilogue: A Love Letter to Self

Mind Attacks

Believe that no matter what happens, you are not alone. I promise to be there for you through your journey. You are enough and have great purpose.

You will need to learn to believe in yourself. It doesn't always come naturally like it does for some people. You will be scared, just like you were in the beginning. There were times it hurt like growing pains, and sometimes it will continue to hurt.

Some people will not be in alignment with you at some point, but it's important to remember that those things that are meant for you can never be taken from you and the people who care for you will cheer you along the way.

I have come to understand that the thing I fear the most is what I need to do. Rejection is a huge fear, but it is only temporary in the process of finding one's true self. Allow yourself time to heal. Thank you for being true to self. I know that it took a lot for you to get to this point.

I commend you for being resilient and dedicated to the transformation of your mind.

Continue to treat yourself as the special person you are. Trust your intuition. Every day, thank the Most High for your blessings and the ones that are yet to come.

Know that you are enough. Rejection does not mean you'll never get what you are striving to achieve. Focus on one day at a time and live for the present. Forgive those who have hurt you, not for them but for you. Your past mistakes don't define who you are today it has made you strong. There is purpose on the other side of your pain.

Give thanks even when things don't go as planned. The road to victory is narrow. Be consistent and present every day. Write down your thoughts. Be mindful of your thoughts!

When you're feeling insecure, remember to say your affirmations and meditate. Forgiveness is key!

Instead of being attacked in your mind choose healing in your heart!

Mind Attacks

If you or someone you know are experiencing any form of abuse, please seek help from one of the national hotlines below.

Childhelp National Child Abuse Hotline
Call 1-800-4-A-CHILD (1-800-422-4453)

Rape, Abuse, and Incest National Network National Sexual Assault Hotline
Hotline: 1 (800) 656-4673

ChildHelp National Child Abuse Hotline
Hotline: 1 (800) 422 – 4453

National Suicide Prevention Lifeline
Hotline: 1-800-273-8255

Sheena McCullough

Sheena McCullough is a Los Angeles Native that's making her way through the authorship journey as a first-time author.

She studied Business Administration at Long Beach City College where she developed a mind for processing information. She has always had a passion and willingness to help others, anyway she possibly could, which lead to her first book being written.

Sheena authored her first book, "Mind Attacks" (launching Sept., 2020) as a way to sympathize with others through personal experiences, while inspiring and motivating others to hold on just a little bit longer while healing is on its way.

She began journaling after she became a mother to her only son. She used him as her inspiration to use her voice. Sheena believes that children have a way of making you feel like you can do anything.

Writing "Mind Attacks" was highly therapeutic for her because it gave her a sense of purpose. Due to her deplorable life experiences, she decided to share her story in hopes that it'll help someone else overcome their battles. Through her journey of healing and overcoming, Sheena has realized the importance of identifying the source and root of your pain and exposing it so that healing can occur.

Sheena plans to author more books, become an advocate and speaker to and for the youth and sexually abused victims. She'd like to encourage them to be a light to others, even when there's been so much darkness in their lives.

Lastly, Sheena has some aspirations of becoming "Dr. McCullough" one day by completing a degree in mental health.

Stay in Touch

www.facebook.com/sheena.leniece

ww.twitter.com/1sheenamac

www.instagram.com/1sheenamac

www.snapchat.com/add/sheenamac.com

www.ingramcontent.com/pod-product-compliance
Lightning Source LLC
Chambersburg PA
CBHW052207090526
44583CB00016BA/1732